Lovely Lucy Prays the Rosary

Lovely Lucy Prays the Rosary

Julianne Weinmann

Illustrated by
Alena Lomkova

2021

Second Printing: 2021

ISBN: 9798557782869

Independently Published

Nokomis, Florida 34275

Website: www.LifetimeWriter.com

Available on Amazon.com

Other books in the *Lovely Lucy* series:
Lovely Lucy's Christmas Dream
The Miracle Mirror

Other *Pray the Rosary* books:
Francisco Prays the Rosary
Lucinta Prays the Rosary

Dedication

Our Lady of the Rosary

Acknowledgements

In appreciation for Christ the King Catholic Church, Sarasota, Florida, where, during worship and Eucharistic Adoration, I am inspired to create books for the glory of God and Our Blessed Lady.

Special thanks to Mary Kuziel, my friend and editor, for her expertise, insights, and prayerful encouragement.

God bless and thank you Father Christopher Mahowald, FSSP, of Christ the King Catholic Church, for his review and editorial comments and contributions.

I am especially grateful for the talent of Alena Lomkova, for her delicate and inspiring watercolor artistry in creating Lovely Lucy and the Fatima scene.

The Rosary beads featured on the prayer pages were made in Jerusalem in the Holy Land.

References and Attributions

Reference notes:
Rosary prayers:
Pray the Rosary with Scripture Readings, A Saint Joseph Edition, Catholic Book Publishing Corp. NJ, 2008
Bible: Holy Bible NRSV The New Revised Standard Version, Catholic Edition, Catholic Bible Press, div. of Thomas Nelson Pub. 1990
Fatima and St. Dominic:
https://www.bluearmy.com/the-story-of-fatima/; https://dominicanfriars.org/about/history-dominican-friars/
The Power of the Rosary (The battle of Lepanto): https://www.tektonministries.org/the-power-of-the-rosary/ and https://www.britannica.com/event/Battle-of-Lepanto

Illustration notes and attributions:
Watercolor paintings: Front and Back Cover (Lovely Lucy and Our Lady of Fatima) and the sign of the cross image of Lucy, by Alena Lomkova.
Rosary Mysteries images licensed from istockphoto.com, photographer: sedmak
Descriptions:
Annunciation: Vienna - The Annunciation paint in presbytery of Salesianerkirche church
by Giovanni Antonio Pellegrini (1725-1727).
Nativity: Turin - The detail of painting of Nativity in Duomo by Giovanni Comandu da Mondovi (1795).
Visitation: Como - The fresco of Visitation fresco in church Santuario del Santissimo Crocifisso
by Gersam Turri.
Presentation: Rome - The Purification of Virgin Mary in the Temple paint in church Chiesa Nuova
(Santa Maria in Vallicella) by Giuseppe Caesari (1568 - 1640).
Finding in the Temple: Sebechleby - Little Jesus teaching in the temple. Fresco from year 1963
by Jozef Antal in st. Michael parish church on August 8, 2013 in Sebechleby, Slovakia.

Olive Tree image PNG Designed By 千图网 from pngtree.com
Statue of Our Lady, licensed from istockphoto.com; photo by Yandry Fernandez
Rose frame "Designed by rawpixel.com / Freepik"
Gold Frame: gorgeous PNG Designed By 姽久 from pngtree.com
Scroll: parchment png image from pngtree.com

To:
From:

The Power of the Rosary

In 1571, in the famous battle of Lepanto,
the naval fleets of Spain, Venice, the Papal states and others,
formed an alliance of Christians to engage the aggressive
Ottoman Empire in the Gulf of Patras in western Greece.
Known as "The Holy League," they joined forces to defeat
the Ottoman Turks, who were expanding their vicious dominance
into the eastern Mediterranean.

In the days leading up to the battle, Pope Pius V
ordered the churches of Rome opened for prayer day and night,
and he encouraged the faithful to ask for the intercession
of the Blessed Virgin Mary by praying the Rosary.
The night before the battle, the Holy League fleet
also prayed the Rosary through the night.

On October 7th, these brave warriors, battling in ships powered by oars,
outnumbered by the enemy, won this fiercesome battle
against the Turks and liberated thousands of enslaved Christians.

Pope Pius V credited victory over the Turks to
Our Lady's intercession through the power of the Rosary.
He established the feast of Our Lady of the Rosary
to be celebrated every year on October 7th to commemorate
her miraculous help in this battle that saved Western Europe.

The Rosary has been instrumental in the conversion of sinners
and many Popes were dedicated to this devotion.

Pray the Rosary every day to harness the power of this beautiful prayer in your life!

Our Lady of Fatima

Long ago, in the year 1916, in Portugal, Spain, the Angel of Peace appeared
to three young shepherd children, Lucia dos Santos, ten years old,
and her cousins, Francisco Marto, nine years old, and Jacinta Marto, seven.
He taught them to pray for peace, in preparation for the vision to come.
A year later, on May 13, 1917, the children again led their sheep to pasture
at the Cova da Iria, the "Cove of Peace." As they prayed near a holm oak tree,
the children were startled by a flash of light. Lucia described the vision:

"A Lady, clothed in white, brighter than the sun,
radiating a light more clear and intense
than a crystal cup filled with sparkling water lit by burning sunlight."
The Lady said to them: "Do not be afraid, I will not harm you."
Lucia asked the Lady: "Where did you come from?"
The Lady answered: "I come from Heaven."

Our Lady told the children many wondrous things.
She asked them to return on the 13th of each month, for six months.
Much of what she said to the children were "secrets,"
only to be revealed to the world in the future.
Our Lady also promised a miracle "… so that all may believe."

The Lady appeared to the children as promised.
On October 13, 1917, the Lady revealed herself to be Our Lady of the Rosary.
She asked the children and all of humanity to
PRAY THE ROSARY EVERY DAY
for peace and to make sacrifices for sinners.

A crowd of about 70,000 people witnessed "The Miracle of the Sun,"
seen from over 20 miles away! Newspapers reported how the sun "danced in the sky,"
swirling and descending toward the earth before it returned to its place in the sky.
Many more wonders occurred. Be sure to read more about this magnificent miracle!

Saint Dominic and the Rosary

Saint Dominic, whose full name was Santo Domingo de Guzmán, was born in Castile, Spain around 1170 and died in Rome, Italy in 1221, at the young age of fifty-one.

As a young man, Dominic was very pious and devout. He sought to serve God more completely and so, during a famine, he sold all of his precious books and possessions, and gave the proceeds to the poor. At age 24, he became a priest. In the year 1215, Dominic established a religious order that would seek to convert souls through preaching and education. They were established as The Order of Preachers, later known by his name, the Dominicans.

He also established a group of women-converts to the monastic life, who were dedicated to praying for Dominic and his preaching companions. Today, the Dominicans include Friars, Nuns, and Lay Fraternities.

In December, 1216, the Pope approved the Order of Preachers. Under Dominic's guidance as Superior, the Order thrived and served throughout Europe.

Beads were used in prayer by many religions for centuries before St. Dominic. But the Rosary as we know it today was first introduced to the world by Saint Dominic.

According to ancient tradition, as Saint Dominic struggled to make conversions to the faith, his preaching fell on deaf ears. He fervently prayed to Our Lady for help and inspiration.

Our Lady appeared to Saint Dominic and told him to pray "the Marian Psalter." This consisted of 150 Hail Mary's and 15 Mysteries, divided into groups: Joyful, Sorrowful, Glorious. The Luminous Mysteries were added later.

The Rosary, as we know it today, evolved from this inspiration.
St. Dominic was devoted to The Blessed Virgin Mary,
who gave the Rosary to the world as a powerful weapon
in the battle against sin and evil.

Prayer Before the Rosary

Queen of the Holy Rosary,
you have deigned to come to Fatima
to reveal to the three shepherd children
the treasures of grace hidden in the Rosary.
Inspire my heart with a sincere love of this devotion,
in order that by meditating on the
Mysteries of our Redemption
which are recalled in it,
we may obtain peace for the world,
the conversion of sinners,
and the favor which I ask of you in this Rosary.

What are YOUR requests and intentions?

I ask it for the greater glory of God, for your own honor,
and for the good of souls, especially for my own.
Amen.

Learn Your Rosary Prayers

The Apostles' Creed

I believe in God, the Father Almighty, creator of Heaven and earth,
and in Jesus Christ, His only Son, Our Lord,
Who was conceived by the Holy Spirit,
born of the Virgin Mary,
suffered under Pontius Pilate,
was crucified, died and was buried.
He descended into hell;
on the third day He rose again from the dead;
He ascended into Heaven,
and is seated at the right hand of God, the Father Almighty;
from thence He shall come to judge the living and the dead.

I believe in the Holy Spirit,
the Holy Catholic Church,
the communion of saints,
the forgiveness of sins,
the resurrection of the body,
and life everlasting.
Amen.

The Lord's Prayer

Our Father, Who art in Heaven,
hallowed be Thy Name.
Thy kingdom come. Thy will be done,
on earth as it is in Heaven.
Give us this day our daily bread,
and forgive us our trepasses, as we forgive
those who trespass against us.
And lead us not into temptation,
but deliver us from evil.
Amen.

The Hail Mary

Hail Mary, full of grace,
the Lord is with thee.
Blessed art thou amongst women,
and blessed is the fruit
of thy womb, Jesus.
Holy Mary, Mother of God,
pray for us sinners,
now and at the hour of our death.
Amen.

Learn Your Rosary Prayers

Glory Be to the Father

Glory Be to the Father, and to the Son,
and to the Holy Spirit.
As it was in the beginning, is now,
and ever shall be,
world without end.
Amen.

Oh My Jesus...

Oh my Jesus,
forgive us our sins.
Save us from the fires of hell.
Lead all souls to heaven,
especially those in most need
of Thy mercy.
Amen.

The 5 Joyful Mysteries

1. The Annunciation
2. The Visitation
3. The Nativity
4. The Presentation
5. The Finding of Jesus in the Temple

of the Most Holy Rosary

of the Blessed Virgin Mary

Begin with the Sign of the Cross:

In the name of the Father,
and of the Son,
and of the Holy Spirit,
Amen.

1
Pray
The Apostles' Creed

I believe in GOD...

2
Pray
The Lord's Prayer

4
Pray
Glory Be to the
Father...

3 Pray
three
Hail Mary's

5 Announce
the 1st Mystery,
"The Annunciation,"
then Pray
The Lord's Prayer

Our Father
Hail Mary
Hail Mary
Hail Mary
Our Father

The First Joyful Mystery
The Annunciation

Pray for the love of humility.

The Angel Gabriel appeared to Mary, a virgin,
who was engaged to Joseph, of the house of David.
The Angel announced to Mary that she will be overshadowed
by the Holy Spirit, and that she will give birth to a holy Child,
who will be the Son of God!

Read Your Bible!
The Gospel According to
LUKE
Chapter 1
Verses 26-38

Then Mary said, "Behold, I am the handmaid of the Lord;
let it be done unto me according to Thy Word."

The Second Joyful Mystery
The Visitation

Pray to love my neighbor.

Mary's cousin Elizabeth was blessed by God in her old age
to bear a son, who will be St. John the Baptist.
He will proclaim the coming of Jesus and baptize sinners unto repentance.
When the Angel Gabriel told Mary this miraculous news,
Mary set out to visit her cousin Elizabeth,
of the house of Zechariah.
Mary stayed with Elizabeth for three months.

Announce
the 2nd Mystery,
then Pray
The Lord's Prayer

Pray
10 Hail Mary's

Pray
Glory Be
to the Father...
then Pray
Oh My Jesus...

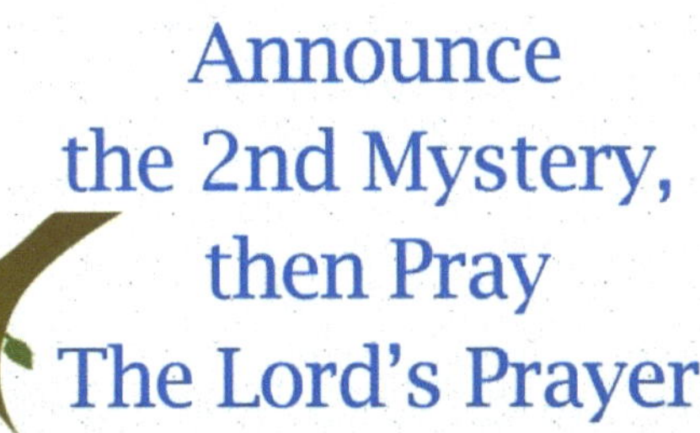

Read Your Bible!

The Gospel According to
LUKE
Chapter 1
Verses 39-56

When Elizabeth heard
Mary's greeting,
the child leaped in her womb.
And Elizabeth was filled with the Holy Spirit
and exclaimed:

"Blessed are you among women,
and blessed is the fruit of your womb."

The Third Joyful Mystery

The Nativity

Pray for the love of God.

In the time of Jesus' birth, there was a decree from the Emperor
that all the world should register.
Joseph took Mary to the city of David called Bethlehem.
While there, Mary gave birth to a Son, Jesus,
and wrapped Him in swaddling clothes and laid Him in a manger
because there was no room for them in the inn.
An angel of God brought the good news to the shepherds in the fields,
who went in haste to glorify and praise Him.

Announce
the 3rd Mystery
then Pray
The Lord's Prayer

Pray
10 Hail Mary's

Pray
Glory Be
to the Father...
then Pray
Oh My Jesus...

Read Your Bible!

The Gospel According to
LUKE
Chapter 2
Verses 1-20

The angel said to the shepherds:
"Do not be afraid; for behold,
I proclaim to you good news of great joy for all people.
For today in the city of David,
a Savior is born,
Who is the Messiah, the Lord."

The Fourth Joyful Mystery
The Presentation in the Temple

Pray for the spirit of obedience and sacrifice.

At the proper time
according to the law,
Joseph and Mary took Jesus
to the Temple in Jerusalem
to present Him for consecration
to the Lord.

They brought with them
an offering of a pair of
turtle doves.

In the meantime,
a man named "Simeon"
was waiting for the Lord's coming,
and The Holy Spirit revealed
to him that he would not die
until he had seen the Messiah!
There was also the prophetess, Anna,
who fortold the coming of a Child
who would be the Redeemer.

Afterward, The Holy Family
returned to Nazareth,
and Jesus grew strong and wise.
God the Father was pleased with Him.

Announce
the 4th Mystery
then Pray
The Lord's Prayer

Pray
10 Hail Mary's

Pray
Glory Be
to the Father...
then Pray
Oh My Jesus...

Read Your Bible!

The Gospel According to
LUKE
Chapter 2
Verses 22-40

Simeon took baby Jesus into his arms,
saying: "Now Master, you can let
your servant go in peace...
for my eyes have seen Thy salvation..."

The Fifth Joyful Mystery

Finding Jesus in the Temple

Pray for the zeal for God's glory.

It was customary for
Jesus, Mary and Joseph to travel
to Jerusalem once a year
for the Feast of the Passover.
When the festivities ended,
Joseph and Mary
began the trip home,
thinking Jesus was somewhere
in the caravan.
But Jesus stayed behind
to sit among the teachers
in the Temple
to listen and ask questions
about the Scriptures.
The teachers were amazed
by this intelligent, holy Boy.

Joseph and Mary
returned to Jerusalem
to search for their Son,
who was twelve years old.
When they found Him,
Jesus reminded them
that, as the Son of God,
He must be in His Father's house.

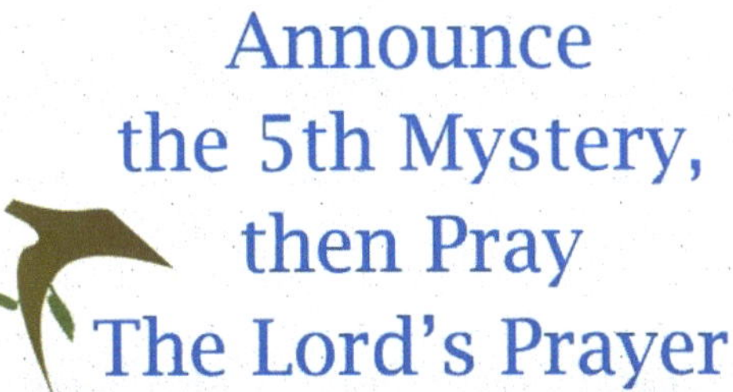

Pray
10 Hail Mary's

Pray
Glory Be
to the Father...
then Pray
Oh My Jesus...

Read Your Bible!
The Gospel According to
LUKE
Chapter 2
Verses 48-50

Prayers
After the
Rosary

When His parents found Him
in the Temple, His mother said to Him:
"Son, why have you done this to us?
Your father and I have been
searching for you with great anxiety."

Jesus answered them:
"Why were you searching for me?
Did you not know that I must be
in my Father's house?"

Prayers After the Rosary

Hail Holy Queen

Hail, holy Queen, Mother of Mercy,
our life, our sweetness, and our hope.
To thee do we cry, poor banished children of Eve.
To thee we send up our sighs,
mourning and weeping in this valley of tears.

Turn then, most gracious Advocate,
thine eyes of mercy towards us;
and after this, our exile,
show unto us the blessed fruit of thy womb, Jesus.
O clement, O loving, O sweet Virgin Mary!

Pray for us, O holy Mother of God,
that we may be made worthy
of the promises of Christ.

Let Us Pray...

O God, whose only-begotten Son,
by His life, death, and resurrection,
has purchased for us the rewards of eternal salvation.
Grant, we beseech Thee,
that while meditating on these mysteries
of the most holy Rosary
of the Blessed Virgin Mary,
we may imitate what they contain
and obtain what they promise,
through the same Christ our Lord.
Amen.

Most Sacred Heart of Jesus,
have mercy on us.
Immaculate Heart of Mary,
pray for us.

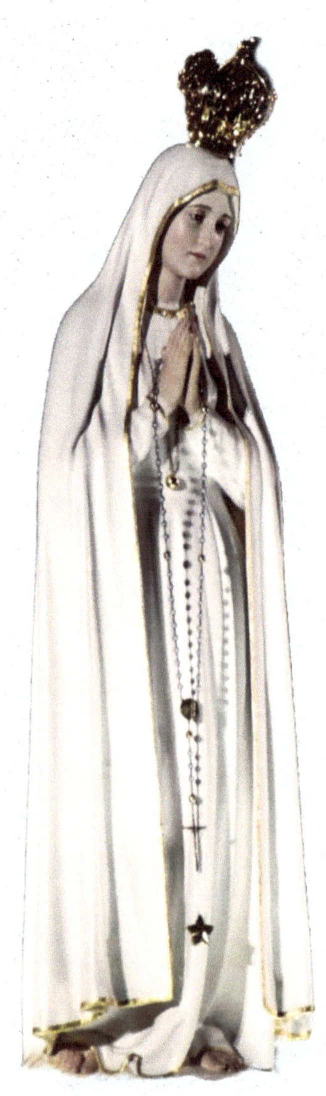

Conclude with the Sign of the Cross:
In the Name of the Father,
and of the Son,
and of the Holy Spirit.
Amen.

The Mysteries of The Holy Rosary

Did You Know?

The Mysteries remind us of the episodes
in the life and death of Our Lord, Jesus Christ.

There are 20 Mysteries of the
Most Holy Rosary of the Blessed Virgin Mary,
grouped into four series:

**The Joyful Mysteries
The Luminous Mysteries
The Sorrowful Mysteries
The Glorious Mysteries**

In this book, Lovely Lucy prays with us
while meditating on The 5 **Joyful** Mysteries.

What are the other 15 Mysteries?

The Luminous Mysteries

1. The Baptism of Jesus
2. The Miracle at Cana
3. The Proclamation of the Kingdom of God
4. The Transfiguration
5. The Institution of the Eucharist

The Sorrowful Mysteries

1. The Agony in the Garden
2. The Scourging at the Pillar
3. The Crowning with Thorns
4. The Carrying of the Cross
5. The Crucifixion

The Glorious Mysteries

1. The Resurrection
2. The Ascension
3. The Descent of the Holy Spirit
4. The Assumption
5. The Coronation of the Blessed Virgin Mary

How many Mysteries can you learn?